Complete Practical Guide on Plantain Flour Processing

By

Benadine Nonye Nduagu

(www.Agric4Profits.com)

Complete Practical Guide on Plantain Flour Processing

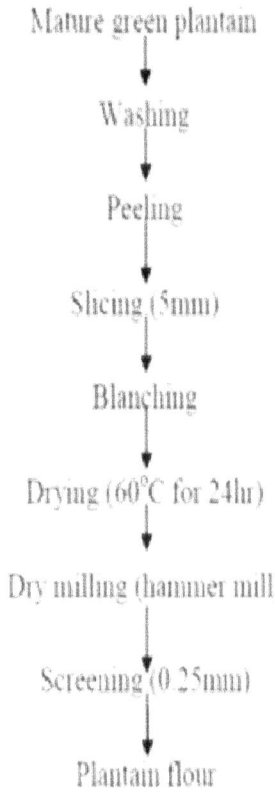

Mature green plantain

↓

Washing

↓

Peeling

↓

Slicing (5mm)

↓

Blanching

↓

Drying (60°C for 24hr)

↓

Dry milling (hammer mill)

↓

Screening (0.25mm)

↓

Plantain flour

The commercial processing of plantain flour involves several steps, starting from the selection of high-quality plantains to the final packaging of the flour.

Here is a detailed explanation of the complete practical process:

1. Selection of Plantains

The selection of high-quality plantains is a critical step in commercial plantain flour processing.

Choose ripe and unblemished plantains for processing. Ideally, select plantains that are yellow with some brown spots, as they are sweeter and have a higher starch content.

Here is a detailed explanation of the practical process involved in selecting plantains:

1. Variety: Choose the appropriate variety of plantains for flour processing. There are different varieties of plantains available, each with its own characteristics and uses.

Some common varieties used for plantain flour production include Horn plantains (Pisang Awak), French plantains (Pisang Klutuk Wulung), and Agbagba plantains.

2. Maturity: Select plantains that are at the right stage of maturity for processing. Plantains used for flour production are usually ripe, as they have higher sugar content and are easier to process.

Look for plantains that are yellow with brown spots, as they indicate ripeness. Green or unripe plantains are less sweet and have a higher starch content, making them more suitable for other culinary purposes.

3. Size and Shape: Consider the size and shape of the plantains. Commercial plantain flour processing typically requires plantains of a uniform size to ensure consistent drying and grinding.

Select plantains that are medium-sized and have a regular shape, as they will be easier to handle during processing.

4. Physical Appearance: Examine the physical appearance of the plantains. Choose plantains that are free from any visible damage, bruises, mold, or insect infestation. Avoid plantains with soft spots or signs of rotting, as they can negatively affect the quality of the flour.

5. Texture: Assess the texture of the plantains. They should be firm to the touch but not overly ripe or mushy. Avoid plantains that are too soft or have a spongy texture, as they may not yield good-quality flour.

6. Ripeness Uniformity: Aim for uniform ripeness among the selected plantains. This ensures that the plantains will have consistent sugar content and starch conversion during the subsequent processing steps.

If there is a mixture of ripe and unripe plantains, it can lead to variations in taste, texture, and color of the final flour.

7. Sourcing: Establish a reliable source for high-quality plantains. Work with reputable farmers, suppliers, or wholesalers who can consistently provide fresh and well-ripened plantains. This helps ensure a steady supply of raw materials for the processing plant.

By following these steps, you can select the best plantains for commercial plantain flour processing. Proper selection of plantains contributes to the overall quality, taste, and nutritional value of the final product.

2. Washing

The washing of plantains is an important step in commercial plantain flour processing to remove dirt, debris, and any surface contaminants.

Thoroughly wash the plantains to remove any dirt or debris. This can be done using clean water or a mild disinfectant solution to ensure hygiene.

Here is a detailed explanation of the practical process involved in washing plantains:

1. Sorting: Before washing, sort the plantains to remove any damaged or spoiled ones. Discard plantains with visible bruises, cuts, or signs of rotting, as they may negatively affect the quality of the flour.

2. Preparing the Washing Area: Set up a clean and dedicated area for washing the plantains. Ensure that the area is well-equipped with running water, sinks, and food-grade cleaning tools such as brushes or scrubbers.

3. Water Supply: Connect a clean water supply to the washing area. The water source should be potable and free from any contaminants. If necessary, use filtration or purification methods to ensure the water's cleanliness.

4. Rinse the Plantains: Place the plantains under running water to rinse off any loose dirt or debris. Hold each plantain individually and rub it gently with your hands to remove any surface impurities. Make sure to rotate the plantains to clean all sides thoroughly.

5. Brushing: For more stubborn dirt or residues, use a clean brush or scrubber to gently scrub the surface of the plantains. Pay particular attention to the crevices and areas around the stem, where dirt may accumulate.

6. Inspect for Quality: While washing, closely inspect the plantains for any remaining dirt, foreign objects, or signs of infestation. Remove any undesirable elements by hand.

7. Repeat if Necessary: If the plantains are heavily soiled or have stubborn dirt, repeat the rinsing and brushing process until they are clean.

8. Drainage: Allow the washed plantains to drain excess water. You can use clean drying racks or place them on clean absorbent surfaces to remove the water.

9. Drying: Ensure that the plantains are completely dry before proceeding with further processing steps. Excess moisture can affect the quality and shelf life of the final flour.

It is crucial to maintain strict hygiene practices throughout the washing process. Here are some additional tips:

- Clean and sanitize the washing area regularly to prevent the buildup of dirt or bacteria.
- Use food-grade cleaning agents if necessary, ensuring that they are properly rinsed off the plantains.
- Wear gloves or use clean utensils when handling the plantains to avoid direct contact with the product.
- Avoid using excessive force or pressure while washing to prevent damaging the plantains.

By following these steps and maintaining proper cleanliness, you can effectively wash the plantains and prepare them for the subsequent stages of commercial plantain flour processing.

3. Peeling

The peeling of plantains is an essential step in commercial plantain flour processing to remove the skins before further processing.

Remove the skins of the plantains. You can use a knife or a mechanical peeler for this process. Ensure that the plantains are peeled completely, leaving no traces of skin.

Here is a detailed explanation of the practical process involved in peeling plantains:

1. Sorting: Before peeling, sort the plantains to ensure that you are working with ripe and suitable plantains for processing. Remove any damaged or spoiled plantains from the batch.

2. Preparing the Peeling Area: Set up a clean and dedicated area for peeling the plantains. Ensure that the area is equipped with a work surface, knives, and waste disposal containers.

3. Cleaning Tools: Make sure that the knives and other peeling tools are clean and sanitized before use. It is essential to maintain hygiene throughout the process to prevent contamination.

4. Cutting the Ends: Start by cutting off both ends of the plantain using a sharp knife. This provides a stable base for the peeling process and allows for easy removal of the skin.

5. Slitting the Skin: With a knife, make a shallow slit lengthwise along the skin of the plantain. Be careful not to cut into the flesh of the plantain. This initial cut helps in loosening the skin and makes the peeling process easier.

6. Peeling the Skin: Hold the plantain firmly and carefully peel off the skin using your hands or the knife. Start from the initial slit and work your way along the length of the plantain. Try to remove the skin in one smooth motion.

7. Repeat for Each Plantain: Repeat the process for each plantain, one at a time, until all the plantains are peeled. Take care to maintain a steady pace while peeling to ensure efficiency.

8. Proper Disposal: Collect the discarded skins in waste disposal containers to maintain cleanliness and prevent any mess in the processing area. Proper waste management is important for maintaining a hygienic work environment.

9. Inspection: While peeling, visually inspect the plantains for any blemishes, bruises, or discoloration. Remove any undesirable portions by cutting them off.

10. Rinse if Needed: If there are any remaining traces of skin or debris on the peeled plantains, rinse them under clean running water to ensure that they are completely clean before proceeding to the next processing step.

Maintaining hygiene throughout the peeling process is crucial. Here are some additional tips:

- Clean and sanitize the peeling area regularly to prevent the buildup of dirt or bacteria.
- Wash hands thoroughly before and after peeling to prevent contamination.
- Use separate cutting boards or surfaces for different batches of plantains to avoid cross-contamination.
- Dispose of the peeled skins properly to prevent attracting pests or creating an unhygienic environment.

By following these steps and maintaining proper cleanliness, you can effectively peel the plantains and prepare them for the subsequent stages of commercial plantain flour processing.

4. Slicing

The slicing of plantains is a crucial step in commercial plantain flour processing to prepare the plantains for further processing, such as blanching and drying.

Slice the peeled plantains into small pieces or chips. The size of the slices can vary depending on the desired texture of the final flour. Thinner slices will result in a finer texture, while thicker slices will give a coarser texture.

Here is a detailed explanation of the practical process involved in slicing plantains:

1. Sorted Plantains: Start with the batch of peeled and sorted plantains that have undergone the peeling process as described earlier. Ensure that the plantains are ripe and suitable for processing.

2. Cutting Surface: Set up a clean and dedicated cutting surface for slicing the plantains. Use a sanitized cutting board or a stainless-steel surface that is easy to clean.

3. Equipment: Prepare a sharp knife or a mechanical slicer suitable for slicing the plantains. Ensure that the equipment is clean and in good working condition.

4. Consistent Thickness: Determine the desired thickness of the plantain slices based on the intended texture of the final flour. The thickness can vary depending on personal preference or market demand.

Generally, thinner slices result in a finer texture, while thicker slices give a coarser texture to the flour.

5. Cutting Technique: Hold a plantain firmly and place it on the cutting surface. Use a knife or a mechanical slicer to slice the plantain evenly into the desired thickness. Ensure that the slices are uniform to ensure consistent drying and grinding.

6. Safety Precautions: When using a knife, exercise caution to prevent any accidental injuries. Follow proper knife handling techniques, such as keeping fingers away from the blade and using a cutting board with a non-slip surface.

7. Repeat the Process: Repeat the slicing process for each plantain, working through the batch systematically. Maintain a steady pace to ensure efficiency.

8. Inspect and Remove Undesirable Parts: While slicing, visually inspect the plantain slices for any remaining blemishes, bruises, or undesirable parts. Remove any such parts using a knife or by hand to ensure that only good-quality slices are used.

9. Proper Handling and Storage: After slicing, handle the plantain slices with care to avoid any damage or contamination. If not proceeding immediately to the next processing step, store the slices properly in clean, food-grade containers or bags to maintain their freshness and quality.

10. Clean-Up: Clean and sanitize the cutting surface, knife, and any other equipment used in the slicing process to prevent cross-contamination and maintain hygiene.

By following these steps and maintaining proper cleanliness, you can effectively slice the plantains and prepare them for the subsequent stages of commercial plantain flour processing.

5. Blanching

Blanching is an essential step in commercial plantain flour processing to soften the plantain slices and prepare them for drying.

Blanch the plantain slices in boiling water for a few minutes. This helps in softening the slices and making them easier to grind. After blanching, drain the water and allow the slices to cool down.

Here is a detailed explanation of the practical process involved in blanching plantains:

1. Prepared Plantain Slices: Start with the batch of sliced plantains that have undergone the slicing process as described earlier. Ensure that the plantain slices are of uniform thickness.

2. Boiling Water: Fill a large pot with clean water and bring it to a boil. The amount of water should be sufficient to fully submerge the plantain slices.

3. Preparing the Blanching Setup: Set up a blanching station with a boiling pot of water, a slotted spoon or a sieve, and a container of cold water. This setup allows for the efficient blanching and cooling of the plantain slices.

4. Blanching Process: Carefully place the plantain slices into the boiling water. Ensure that the water covers the slices completely.

Depending on the quantity being processed, it may be necessary to blanch the plantain slices in batches to avoid overcrowding the pot.

5. Timing: Blanch the plantain slices for about 2-3 minutes. This time is sufficient to soften the slices without overcooking them.

6. Testing for Readiness: After the blanching time, test the readiness of the plantain slices by taking out a sample slice and pressing it gently. It should be slightly soft but still retain its shape.

Overcooking can lead to the slices becoming mushy and difficult to handle during the drying process.

7. Removal from Boiling Water: Once the plantain slices are blanched, remove them from the boiling water using a slotted spoon or a sieve. Shake off any excess water to ensure proper draining.

8. Plunging into Cold Water: Immediately transfer the blanched plantain slices into a container of cold water. This cold water bath stops the cooking process and helps retain the bright color of the slices. Leave the slices in the cold water for a few minutes.

9. Draining: Drain the cooled plantain slices thoroughly to remove any excess water. You can use a colander, sieve, or clean absorbent cloth to aid in the drainage process. Proper draining is important to facilitate efficient drying.

10. Proceed to Dry: Once the plantain slices are properly drained, they are ready for the drying process as described in the previous explanations.

The blanched slices should be dried until they become crispy and brittle, with a moisture content of around 8-10%.

Remember to maintain hygiene throughout the blanching process. Here are some additional tips:

- Clean and sanitize the blanching equipment, including the pot, slotted spoon or sieve, and containers used for cold water.
- Ensure that the blanching pot and utensils are free from any residual dirt or debris.
- Work in batches if necessary to avoid overcrowding the pot and to ensure proper blanching of the plantain slices.

By following these steps and maintaining proper cleanliness, you can effectively blanch the plantain slices and prepare them for the subsequent drying process in commercial plantain flour processing.

6. Drying

Drying is a crucial step in commercial plantain flour processing that removes the moisture from the blanched plantain slices, ensuring their long-term storage and preservation.

There are multiple methods for drying plantain slices. The traditional method involves sun-drying the slices on clean mats or racks in a well-ventilated area.

However, for commercial processing, mechanical drying methods such as using hot air dryers or dehydrators are more efficient and consistent.

The slices should be dried until they become crispy and brittle, with a moisture content of around 8-10%.

Here is a detailed explanation of the practical process involved in drying plantains:

1. Prepared Plantain Slices: Start with the batch of blanched plantain slices that have undergone the blanching process as described earlier. Ensure that the slices are properly blanched and drained.

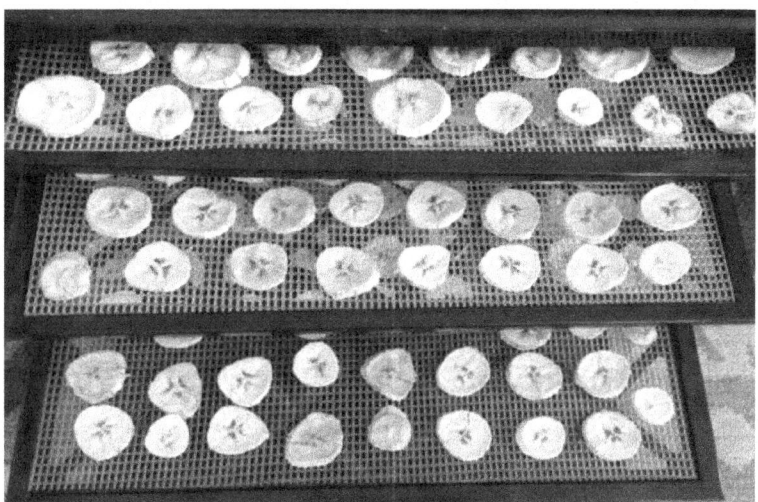

2. Select Drying Method: There are different methods for drying plantain slices in commercial plantain flour processing. The two main methods are:

a. Sun Drying: Traditionally, plantain slices are spread out on clean mats or racks in a well-ventilated area exposed to direct sunlight. However, this method is weather-dependent and may not be suitable in areas with high humidity or frequent rainfall.

b. Mechanical Drying: In modern commercial processing, mechanical drying methods are preferred for their efficiency and consistency. Hot air dryers or dehydrators are used to control temperature, humidity, and drying time.

3. Preparing the Drying Setup: For sun drying, arrange clean and sanitized drying mats or racks in an area with ample sunlight. Ensure that the drying surface is free from dust or dirt. For mechanical drying, set up the hot air dryer or dehydrator according to the manufacturer's instructions.

4. Spreading the Plantain Slices: For sun drying, spread the blanched plantain slices evenly on the drying mats or racks. Avoid overlapping the slices to ensure uniform drying.

For mechanical drying, place the slices on the trays or racks of the hot air dryer or dehydrator, leaving space between the slices for proper airflow.

5. Drying Process: In sun drying, expose the plantain slices to direct sunlight and natural airflow. Turn the slices occasionally to ensure even drying. The drying time can vary depending on the weather conditions and thickness of the slices but may take several days.

In mechanical drying, set the hot air dryer or dehydrator to a temperature of around 60-70°C (140-158°F). The drying time will depend on the dryer's capacity and the thickness of the slices, but it typically ranges from 6 to 12 hours.

6. Monitoring: Regularly monitor the drying progress to prevent over-drying or under-drying. The plantain slices should be dried until they become crispy and brittle, with a moisture content of around 8-10%.

7. Cooling: After drying, allow the plantain slices to cool down to room temperature before further processing. This helps prevent condensation and moisture buildup in the final product.

8. Conditioning (Optional): For improved storage stability, conditioning can be done by placing the dried plantain slices in clean, airtight containers for a few days. This helps distribute any remaining moisture evenly within the slices.

9. Milling/Grinding: Once the dried plantain slices have cooled down and undergone conditioning (if applicable), they are ready for milling or grinding. Use a hammer mill, pin mill, or commercial grinder to achieve the desired particle size for the plantain flour.

10. Sieving: After grinding, sieve the plantain flour to remove any coarse particles or impurities. This ensures a smooth and consistent texture of the final plantain flour.

11. Packaging: Package the plantain flour in moisture-proof materials to protect it from humidity and external contaminants. Label the packages with relevant information such as product name, weight, nutritional information, and expiration date.

12. Storage: Store the packaged plantain flour in a cool, dry place away from direct sunlight. Proper storage conditions help maintain the quality, flavor, and nutritional value of the flour.

By following these steps and maintaining proper hygiene throughout the drying process, you can effectively dry the plantain slices and produce high-quality plantain flour in commercial plantain flour processing.

7. Milling/Grinding

The milling or grinding of dried plantain slices is a crucial step in commercial plantain flour processing, as it transforms the dried slices into a fine powder, which is the final product, plantain flour.

Once the plantain slices are properly dried, they need to be ground into a fine powder to obtain plantain flour.

You can use a hammer mill, pin mill, or commercial grinder to achieve this. The milling process should be carefully controlled to maintain a consistent texture and particle size.

Here is a detailed explanation of the practical process involved in milling or grinding plantains:

1. Dried Plantain Slices: Start with the batch of dried plantain slices that have undergone the drying process as described earlier. Ensure that the slices are completely dried, crispy, and free from excess moisture.

2. Milling Equipment: Select the appropriate milling or grinding equipment based on the scale of your commercial plantain flour processing operation. Commonly used equipment includes hammer mills, pin mills, and commercial grinders. The choice of equipment depends on factors such as production capacity, desired particle size, and budget.

3. Cleaning the Equipment: Before use, ensure that the milling equipment is clean and free from any residual particles or contaminants. Proper cleaning and sanitation are essential to prevent any cross-contamination and maintain food safety standards.

4. Setting the Milling Parameters: Set the milling parameters based on the desired texture and particle size of the plantain flour. The milling equipment may have adjustable settings for speed, feed rate, and screen size to achieve the desired results.

5. Loading the Equipment: Carefully load the dried plantain slices into the milling equipment. For larger commercial operations, this may be done using conveyor systems or hoppers for efficient and continuous processing.

6. Milling/Grinding Process: Turn on the milling equipment and feed the dried plantain slices into the machine. The equipment will break down the slices into small particles or powder through a combination of impact, compression, and shearing forces.

7. Monitoring the Process: Regularly monitor the milling process to ensure that the plantain slices are ground to the desired particle size. Depending on the equipment and settings, this process can take a few minutes to an hour or more.

8. Collecting the Flour: As the plantain slices are ground, the resulting flour or powder will be collected in a receptacle or container below the milling equipment. Make sure that the collection area is clean and free from any contamination.

9. Repeat as Necessary: Continue the milling process until all the dried plantain slices have been ground into flour. Depending on the batch size and the capacity of the milling equipment, this may be done in several batches.

10. Sieving (Optional): If a very fine texture is desired, the plantain flour can be sieved using different mesh sizes to remove any remaining coarse particles or impurities. This step helps achieve a smoother and more uniform texture in the final flour.

11. Packaging: Package the plantain flour in moisture-proof materials to protect it from humidity and external contaminants. Label the packages with relevant information such as product name, weight, nutritional information, and expiration date.

12. Storage: Store the packaged plantain flour in a cool, dry place away from direct sunlight. Proper storage conditions help maintain the quality, flavor, and nutritional value of the flour.

By following these steps and maintaining proper hygiene throughout the milling process, you can effectively produce high-quality plantain flour in commercial plantain flour processing.

8. Sieving

Sieving is an important step in commercial plantain flour processing that helps achieve a smoother and more uniform texture by removing any remaining coarse particles or impurities.

After grinding, sieve the plantain flour to remove any coarse particles or impurities. This will result in a smoother and more uniform flour. The flour can be sieved using different mesh sizes depending on the desired fineness.

Here is a detailed explanation of the practical process involved in sieving plantain flour:

1. Prepared Plantain Flour: Start with the batch of plantain flour that has undergone the milling or grinding process as described earlier. The flour may contain small particles of varying sizes.

2. Select Sieves: Choose the appropriate sieves based on the desired fineness of the plantain flour. Sieves with different mesh sizes can be used to achieve varying levels of refinement. The mesh size is determined by the number of holes per square inch or centimeter.

3. Clean and Sanitize: Before using the sieves, make sure they are clean and sanitized. Proper cleaning is essential to prevent any contamination and maintain the quality of the plantain flour.

4. Set Up the Sieving Area: Arrange the sieving equipment in a clean and designated area. This area should be free from any contaminants that may affect the quality of the flour.

5. Double Sieving (Optional): For improved refinement, you may perform a double sieving process. In this case, use a coarse sieve first to remove larger particles, and then pass the flour through a finer sieve to achieve a smoother texture.

6. Pouring the Plantain Flour: Place the plantain flour on top of the sieve(s). Use a ladle or scoop to ensure a consistent and even layer of flour on the surface of the sieve.

7. Sieving Process: Gently shake or tap the sieve to pass the flour through the mesh. Coarse particles and impurities will be retained on top of the sieve, while the finer flour will fall through into a clean container placed below the sieve.

8. Checking Sieved Flour: Periodically check the residue on top of the sieve to see if any larger particles or impurities need to be removed.

9. Re-sieving (Optional): If using a double-sieving process, transfer the residue from the coarse sieve to a finer sieve and repeat the sieving process to further refine the flour.

10. Packaging: Package the sieved plantain flour in moisture-proof materials to protect it from humidity and external contaminants. Label the packages with relevant information such as product name, weight, nutritional information, and expiration date.

11. Storage: Store the packaged plantain flour in a cool, dry place away from direct sunlight. Proper storage conditions help maintain the quality, flavor, and nutritional value of the flour.

By following these steps and maintaining proper hygiene throughout the sieving process, you can effectively produce high-quality and refined plantain flour in commercial plantain flour processing.

9. Packaging

Packaging is a critical step in commercial plantain flour processing as it protects the flour from moisture, contaminants, and physical damage, ensuring its quality and shelf life.

Once the plantain flour is ready, it needs to be properly packaged to maintain its quality and shelf life. Use moisture-proof packaging materials such as food-grade polyethylene bags or laminated pouches to protect the flour from moisture and external contaminants.

Label the packages with necessary information such as product name, weight, nutritional information, and expiration date.

Here is a detailed explanation of the practical process involved in packaging plantain flour:

1. Prepared Plantain Flour: Start with the batch of sieved and refined plantain flour that has undergone the sieving process as described earlier. Ensure that the flour is smooth, free from coarse particles, and ready for packaging.

2. Select Packaging Materials: Choose suitable packaging materials for the plantain flour. Common options include food-grade polyethylene bags, laminated pouches, or paper bags with inner liners. The selected materials should be moisture-proof and provide a barrier against external contaminants.

3. Cleaning and Sanitization: Before starting the packaging process, clean and sanitize the packaging area and all tools involved, such as scoops, weighing scales, and sealing machines. This ensures the hygiene and safety of the final product.

4. Weighing and Measuring: Weigh the required amount of plantain flour for each package, depending on the specified weight or volume indicated on the packaging. Use accurate weighing scales to ensure consistency in each package.

5. Filling the Packaging: Carefully transfer the measured plantain flour into the chosen packaging material. For better precision and cleanliness, use scoops or funnels during this process. Be cautious not to spill or contaminate the flour during filling.

6. Removing Air and Sealing: Remove any excess air from the packaging to prevent spoilage and extend the shelf life of the flour. Depending on the packaging material, use heat sealing, zip-lock closures, or other appropriate methods to secure the package.

7. Quality Control: Regularly inspect the packaged flour for any signs of contamination, damage, or incorrect weight. Address any issues promptly to maintain product quality and consistency.

8. Labeling: Each package should be labeled with essential information, including product name, weight, nutritional information, allergen warnings, manufacturing date, and expiration date. Proper labeling helps consumers identify and use the product correctly.

9. Batch Coding: Assign a unique batch code to each packaging batch. This allows for traceability and helps identify the production date and other relevant information in case of any quality issues.

10. Storage and Stacking: Once packaged, store the plantain flour in a clean and designated storage area. Stack the packages neatly, leaving enough space for proper ventilation and easy access.

11. Cleaning Up: After packaging is complete, clean and sanitize the packaging area and equipment to maintain a hygienic processing environment.

12. Quality Assurance: Regularly conduct quality checks on the packaging materials, seals, and labeling to ensure they meet the required standards and comply with food safety regulations.

By following these steps and adhering to proper hygiene practices, you can effectively package plantain flour in a commercial plantain flour processing facility, ensuring that the product remains fresh, safe, and of high quality for consumers.

10. Storage

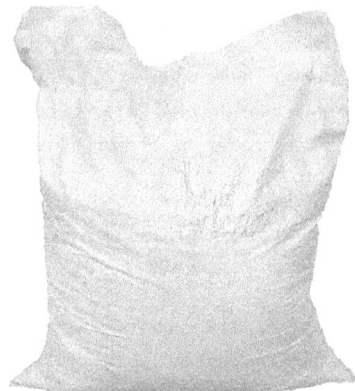

The storage of plantains is a crucial step in commercial plantain flour processing to maintain their freshness and quality until they are ready for further processing.

Store the packaged plantain flour in a cool, dry place away from direct sunlight. Proper storage conditions help maintain the quality, flavor, and nutritional value of the flour.

It's important to note that the specific equipment and techniques used may vary depending on the scale of the processing plant and available resources.

Additionally, adherence to food safety standards, quality control measures, and local regulations are crucial throughout the entire process to ensure the production of safe and high-quality plantain flour.

Here is a detailed explanation of the practical process involved in the storage of plantain flour:

1. Sorting and Cleaning: Before storage, sort the plantains again to remove any damaged or spoiled ones. Only store ripe and healthy plantains that are suitable for processing. Thoroughly clean the plantains to remove any dirt or debris.

2. Preparing the Storage Area: Set up a dedicated and clean storage area for the plantains. The storage area should be well-ventilated, dry, and away from direct sunlight. It should also be free from any potential contaminants that may affect the quality of the plantains.

3. Temperature and Humidity: Maintain the storage area at a temperature of around 12-15°C (54-59°F) and a relative humidity of 65-70%. These conditions help slow down the ripening process and prevent mold growth.

4. Storing in Baskets or Crates: Arrange the cleaned plantains in baskets or crates in a single layer to allow for proper air circulation. Avoid stacking the plantains, as it can lead to bruising and accelerate ripening.

5. Inspection: Regularly inspect the stored plantains for any signs of ripening, mold, or damage. Remove any overripe or spoiled plantains immediately to prevent the spread of spoilage.

6. Ethylene Absorbent Packs (Optional): To further slow down the ripening process, you may consider using ethylene absorbent packs placed strategically within the storage area. Ethylene is a natural ripening agent produced by fruits, and these packs can help absorb excess ethylene, extending the shelf life of the plantains.

7. Monitoring: Continuously monitor the temperature and humidity levels in the storage area to ensure they remain within the optimal range. Regularly check the plantains for any changes in condition.

8. Rotation: Practice first-in, first-out (FIFO) inventory management to ensure that older batches of plantains are used first, reducing the risk of spoilage.

9. Proper Handling: When handling the stored plantains, be gentle to avoid bruising or damaging the fruit.

10. Storage Duration: Depending on the maturity of the plantains at the time of storage and the storage conditions, plantains can be stored for several days to a few weeks before they are processed into plantain flour.

By following these steps and maintaining proper storage conditions, you can effectively preserve the freshness and quality of the plantains until they are ready for further processing in commercial plantain flour processing. Proper storage ensures that the plantains remain suitable for producing high-quality plantain flour.